HOW TO HYPNOTIZE YOURSELF INTO HAPPINESS

JASON CHRISTOPHER

Printed and Bound in the United States of America.

First Printing 2017

HOW TO HYPNOTIZE YOURSELF INTO HAPPINESS

CONTENTS

INTRODUCTION

ARE you fascinated by hypnosis? Wondering if what you saw during a stage show or felt in a therapist's office could actually be real? That's completely understandable – I'm still fascinated by it, and I see someone go into a hypnotic trance every week.

Let me start this short book by answering the first question that's usually on someone's mind when they speak to a hypnotist: *yes, hypnosis is real.* Good stage hypnotists aren't using actors, and you really can quit smoking, get over your fear of flying, or reach a difficult goal using the power of the mind.

In fact, that takes me to the next thing I want you to know, and its a detail that's a lot more important: you can use aspects of hypnotism to change your life. What's more, it's an easy, inexpensive, and effective way to reach a goal. When you change your mind, you really do change your life.

This shouldn't be all that surprising. You already know how differently you can react to something when you're in a good mood versus a bad mood. The way you feel about someone colors the way you react to their actions and statements. Things you might tolerate or even enjoy about a loved one, a politician you like, or a favorite athlete or actor could seem annoying or unforgivable in a professional rival, a political opponent, or public personality you can't stand. In hundreds of studies, doctors have observed that placebo sugar pills are often as effective as real medication.

In each of these cases, what we have is a situation in which the way you think or feel about something influences your reality. In a state of hypnosis the same thing happens, but on a deeper level. Deeply-held beliefs and associations can be changed. New habits can be forged. Goals that used to seem impossibly far away can suddenly come into reach.

How could a change of mental perspective improve your life? What is it about hypnosis that can actually make you happier, and how can you use it? Throughout the rest of this short book, I'm going to give you those answers. Better yet, I'm going to provide them in as simple and straightforward a way as possible. While there is a lot of deep psychological research behind the phenomenon of hypnosis, the reality is that you don't need to know it in order to live a happier, more successful life. Just as you don't need to know all of the mechanical details of your car's engine in order to drive to work, you can alter your own thoughts and feelings with just a few proven mental strategies.

I promise that the information I have to share can help you to get more out of every day if you're willing to keep an open mind and give the advice a try. So, if you're ready to uncover some of the magic of hypnosis – and better yet, put it to work in your own life – then let's get started!

CHAPTER ONE:

IT'S UP TO YOU TO CHANGE YOUR LIFE

ONE of the most popular fantasies people have is winning the lottery. Who hasn't daydreamed about suddenly coming into a few million dollars in the blink of an eye?

Thinking about these kinds of dreams can be fun for a few minutes at a time, especially in the midst of a dreary work day. However, they point to one of the biggest reasons most adults have a hard time following through on their goals and wishes: they want some external miracle to push them in the right direction. They would be a lot more likely to get where they were going if they would just put in some small but consistent effort.

In other words, while you aren't likely to hit the jackpot anytime soon, mathematically speaking, you are almost guaranteed to achieve financial security if you make a reasonable plan, save some money, and get smart about things like investments and taxes.

You can get all the money you want either by saving or by becoming lucky in an instant, but only one of those options is under your control. If you leave it to chance, or the world at large, many of your dreams are probably going to be unfulfilled. That's something most of us come to understand pretty early on in life, but we don't always act on this understanding. However, if you're going to get the most from this short book on hypnosis, it's something you absolutely have to grasp and internalize.

Hypnosis is About Shifting Mental Perspectives

When I hypnotize someone, whether on a stage or in a therapy setting, it appears that I'm doing something *to* them. It's closer to the truth, however, to say that a hypnotist and a subject are working together to create the same result. In a comedy routine, for instance, it's the hypnotic subjects who are really the stars. Their reactions and behaviors are what get the big laughs. The performer is just setting the stage so that the right things can happen.

It's the same with this book, or any piece of self-help advice. What I can offer you is a new way of thinking that makes it possible for you to achieve what's important. What I *can't* do, though, is put the new way of thinking to work for you.

You still have to decide who you want to be and how you want to live, and then take the first steps so that what I teach you can be useful.

When you start thinking differently about yourself and the world around you, truly amazing things can happen. That's not just a piece of motivational fluff – it's actually supported by science, and I can prove it.

Stop what you're doing for a moment and take a walk down the street your home or office is on. As you do, count the number of signs you see. Try to be as exact as possible, and don't miss any. Then come back and keep reading.

Did you count many different signs? If so, you probably noticed something: there were likely more signs than you would have thought your familiar street had. By simply being aware of them, you noticed things that wouldn't have otherwise stood out to you. You paid attention to signs that would have faded into the background if you were not actually looking for them.

Now take this exercise one step further. Without going out again, try to remember how many dogs, cars, or people you passed. I'll bet your memories of these are much less sharp. That's only natural – you were focusing your attention on something else.

This works for both small examples and big changes in our lives. The more carefully we are dialed in on a certain type of thought or feeling, the more receptive we become to it. In the same way that a hypnotic subject can be intensely concentrated on a suggestion I've offered, your mind can become fixated on a certain goal or idea.

One piece of advice therapists often give to clients who are depressed or discouraged is to start a gratitude journal. The patient simply lists a few things every day that they are thankful for. What's interesting about this is that keeping a journal doesn't actually change any events or circumstances in the person's life. And yet, they inevitably began to feel happier and better right away. It's easy to see why. Suddenly, they are aware of all the things that are going right in their life, rather than dwelling on all that is wrong.

If you want to feel better than you do now, or do something differently than you've done it in the past, you have to change the way you think and feel about it first.

Everything Starts With a Decision

As I pointed out before, most people have wishes and daydreams that revolve around wealth, fame, or achievement. What most of them don't have, though, are firm plans and real goals.

The big difference, of course, is a matter of commitment. If you *wish* you were rich, you can buy a lottery ticket, get your hopes up for a few hours, and then forget about it. If you daydream about being in great shape, you can fantasize about your beach-ready body, but then go back to eating junk food. But if you become serious about any of these things, you have to make a plan. That might involve learning, sacrifice, and even disappointment.

Is it any wonder, then, that so many people choose wishing over action? Having daydreams is fun and immediately satisfying. Committing to a change in your life calls for work, ongoing effort, and has the potential for failure. In the end, though, it's the only way to get at the things you really want. You have to decide you're going to take on a challenge and then work to make it real.

In some ways, this can be the hardest part of the process. When you decide you're really serious about pursuing what's important to you, forward progress becomes a possibility. Hypnosis can help move things along, but it can't replace a real sense of desire, or at least not for very long. By tapping into your subconscious mind, I can temporarily convince you to do, believe, or act upon a lot of different suggestions. But in order for them to be sustainable you have to believe you actually want them.

All of us are influenced by our genetics, our surroundings, and the mental inputs (such as the books and articles we read) we experience every day. Not all of those factors get equal weight, though. We are most drawn to that which appeals to us emotionally. Make the decision now to start chasing after the goals that make you feel happier and more fulfilled. You won't just get more satisfaction from the results; you'll also have an easier time going forward.

One reason hypnotism is so effective in changing behavior is that we are all driven by, and susceptible to, ongoing mental loops. We tend to see what we expect to see, and hear what we want to hear. So, when things are moving in a positive direction, we learn to anticipate more positivity. Likewise, when we fill our minds with negativity, it seems as if bad news and setbacks are coming at us from every angle. This comes back to the idea of focus and awareness, and it can affect our moods and achievements at every moment and level of our lives.

We've all known people who seem to have nothing but good luck, as well as those who suffer one misfortune after another. Not all of these factors are mental, of course, but our beliefs and mindsets carry more weight than you might imagine. The first step to creating change is making the decision to do so. Are you ready?

Using Hypnotism to Take the Next Step

In the next chapter, I'm going to introduce some simple facts and ideas about hypnotism so you can better understand what it's about and how your subconscious mind works. But once again, let me point out that it's only going to be effective for you if you're willing to make changes to your thinking and behavior.

On a stage or in a therapy session, I can guide a person through relaxation and visualization techniques that leave them in a deeply focused state. But these techniques won't work unless they are willing to relax and focus in the first place. It's the same with this book. You can reprogram yourself for success and achievement, but it won't happen automatically just because you read the pages. Instead, you have to make the commitment to try something new, and to keep practicing until you see results.

It's a great honor for me to be able to work with people for the purposes of entertainment and self-improvement. In every case, I remind them that the outcomes are more dependent on their willingness to participate than my talent. It really is up to you to take control of your own life. Once you decide to do that, hypnosis can be a powerful mental catalyst that keeps you moving in the right direction.

CHAPTER TWO:

GOING DEEPER INTO YOUR MIND

ONE of the great ironies in life is that most people don't have a clear picture of the way their minds work. They are flooded with thoughts, dreams, and anxieties all day long, but never really stop to think about the mental machinery needed to put them in motion.

I won't claim to know everything about the human brain. What I do know and understand, however, can be useful for understanding just why we cling to the beliefs and behaviors we do... and more importantly, what's needed to change them once and for all.

The first step down that road is accepting that in many ways you actually have two minds. This doesn't mean you have a split personality or some other imbalance, just that different parts of your brain are assigned to different tasks.

Meeting the Two Parts of Your Mind

If you've ever taken a psychology course, you may already be aware that you have a conscious and subconscious mind. You might have even learned some of the more intense theories about the subconscious and how it relates to fears and dreams.

That's all very interesting, and it can lead to some outlandish Hollywood plotlines. In a day-to-day sense, though, your subconscious mind has a much more mundane existence. Basically, it's tasked with helping you remember who you are and what you have to do to stay alive.

For instance, you don't have to consciously think about breathing, or concentrate to make your heart beat. You couldn't do so even if you tried. Your conscious mind doesn't have to be involved when it's time to digest food, fall asleep, or scratch a spot on the top of your head. In fact, you can do a lot of things, like driving and walking, with little or no conscious thought at all. That frees up more powerful parts of your brain to decide what to wear, perform advanced calculus, or write a book like this one.

We couldn't function as self-aware beings without both parts of our minds working together in harmony. However, sometimes the two halves disagree, and when that happens the results might not be exactly what you would expect.

Your Two Minds Work Together, But One is Stronger

It would be reasonable to assume that your conscious mind is more powerful than your subconscious. After all, it is bigger and newer. Humans didn't develop their large brains until relatively recently in our genetic history, and it takes a lot more mental horsepower to pass a college class, for example, than it does to sit in a chair without falling over.

The interesting reality is that things work in the exact opposite way as you might expect. When your conscious mind wants one thing and the subconscious wants another, the deeper and older parts of your brain will win out every time. That's because survival, and the feeling of safety, always overpowers conscious thought. You can try to hold your breath until you pass out or go days without sleeping, but most of the time your subconscious will kick in and overrule you.

I can give you two quick examples that perfectly show this dynamic at work. The first has to do with dieting and exercise. Millions and millions of us decide to shed a few extra pounds every year. More often than not, we end up falling back into old habits. That's largely because our subconscious minds feel safer eating what we always eat, and avoiding the pain of exercise, than they do adopting new routines and habits. Your subconscious thinks you can survive just fine by sticking to established patterns, so it doesn't like to break them. Even if your conscious self wants to look great in a bathing suit, your subconscious will win unless you point it in another direction.

For a more obvious visual, you can see what happens in a state of hypnosis. Although I'll go into more detail in the next chapter, a hypnotized person is one who is essentially listening with their subconscious mind instead of their conscious brain. If you convince the inner mind that it's a chicken, it will start to cluck accordingly. That idea might be ridiculous to the conscious brain, but that doesn't matter – the subconscious always wins.

That can seem like bad news, especially if you've gone through several unsuccessful diets, or have failed in your conscious plans and ideas in the past. But contained within these mental roadblocks are the keys to overcoming common obstacles. If you can convince your subconscious to adopt a certain change, then your actions and habits will naturally follow.

Let's go back to an example I gave a moment ago. A hypnotized person who clucks like a chicken believes, in that short moment, that they are in fact a piece of poultry. That effect doesn't last for long. However, by using more powerful forms of hypnosis – either by yourself or with the help of a professional – you can affect permanent mental changes.

What if you saw yourself as a person who loved to eat healthy foods and work out regularly? Imagine if you could train your mind to accept the notion that you are a non-smoker who no longer craved cigarettes. How would it feel if you could defeat a fear of flying, the anxiety of taking tests, or some other nagging problem?

In each case, altering your subconscious mind could allow you to make almost instant changes in your habits and behavior. It's simple science: when you see yourself as fit and healthy, for example, you'll begin to make the kinds of decisions a fit and healthy person would.

How to Change Your Mental Programming

When people start to accept the idea that the subconscious mind can be changed in positive ways, they often become eager to "flip a switch" and adopt a whole new set of qualities and habits. Essentially, they want to hack their own minds to be super healthy, productive, and motivated.

Unfortunately, it's not usually quite that simple. Although using hypnosis to alter subconscious thoughts and beliefs is quick, easy, and affordable, it's not the kind of thing that is usually accomplished in 15 or 20 minutes. There certainly *are* people who are very suggestible, and those who have a true desire to change will respond to hypnosis quickly. In most cases, though, a little bit of sustained effort is needed.

There are couple of reasons for this. The first has to do with the fact that your subconscious mind is protected. Because it's such a powerful part of your own brain, it's important that only the right thoughts and ideas get through. Most of what comes into your conscious mind will be rejected on a deeper level. In psychology, they call this phenomenon the "critical factor," and it stops you from believing or acting upon everything you hear. It might be convenient to do so, but it wouldn't be very good for your survival, and it's important to remember that keeping you safe is what the subconscious is all about.

Again, this has both a positive and a negative element. While it might be hard to change your subconscious quickly, it's also true that once you accept a positive belief or idea you're likely to stick with it. To put it another way, you might feel like it's impossible to give up salty or sugary foods today, but once you retrain your inner mind to want healthier options you'll stop craving junk food altogether. If you can do what's needed to improve your life (which isn't that hard to begin with), you'll probably retain those habits forever.

There are a few different pathways into the subconscious. The most obvious probably isn't going to help you. That's because our subconscious minds absorb new information and ideas most readily when we are very young. The things we learn from our parents and our childhood experiences tend to make a very strong impression. We become less malleable as we age, though, starting with our teenage years.

The next way to influence your subconscious is through repetition. Anything you hear again and again is likely to eventually be internalized by some part of your deeper brain. Hear someone tell you you're attractive often enough and you'll begin to believe it. Or get the message that you aren't smart enough to succeed, and you'll probably begin to feel that, too.

Another way to influence your subconscious mind is through emotion. You probably remember where you were during certain vivid and powerful moments of your life. Most adults can vividly recall meeting someone who made their heart skip a beat, or where they were when they heard the news about a tragedy. The strong emotions associated with these events make them memorable and powerful. They influence our subconscious selves in ways that facts, statistics, and rational ideas can't.

And finally, you can change your subconscious through the use of hypnosis. In many ways, hypnosis is simply the combination of each of these other tools. It draws on emotion and repetition, while helping you to bypass the critical factor in your mind through focusing and relaxation techniques. In essence, it lets you communicate directly with your subconscious so you can start controlling what it is you think and believe most deeply.

Now that you have a framework for thinking about your subconscious, and an understanding of why it's such a powerful predictor of your behavior, let's move on to the main event and see how hypnosis really works.

CHAPTER THREE:

HOW HYPNOSIS REALLY WORKS

Although the workings of the subconscious mind can be fascinating in their own right, you were probably tempted to skip ahead to this chapter and start reading about the details of hypnosis. I hope you didn't, though, because you can't really properly understand the hypnotic phenomenon without grasping the fact that the subconscious mind is more powerful than your conscious brain. The latter might be bigger and more complex, but the subconscious gets veto power, and that's where hypnosis comes in.

That's because hypnosis is essentially a mental shortcut. It allows us to bypass that critical factor and communicate directly with the subconscious mind. In that state, we can change thoughts, beliefs, and emotional impressions. In some situations, those changes will be temporary and chosen for entertainment value, like when a hypnotist makes you cluck like a chicken onstage. In more therapeutic settings, they can be used to undo psychological damage, change deeply ingrained habits, and open up a new world of possibilities.

You've probably seen countless movies where the heroes need to slip into a base, building, or research facility that's heavily guarded. Often, they'll create some kind of distraction (usually an explosion or a plan involving elaborate costumes) that allows them to slip in undetected. In some ways, hypnosis is like that. It's the practice of occupying or bypassing the conscious mind so real work can be done at a deeper level.

So that you can better understand this process as you see or experience it, this chapter will be devoted to a few facts on the way hypnosis really works.

Hypnosis is a Natural State

Often, audience members at a comedy hypnosis show tend to think of a hypnotist as doing something that's mystical or outlandish. In reality, what you are seeing is a trained professional or performer using scientific techniques to induce a completely natural state.

In other words, all of us can be hypnotized. In fact, we spend more time in a state of hypnosis than we usually imagine. If you've ever found yourself "spacing out" while daydreaming, watching a television program, or driving on a long stretch of highway, then you've been hypnotized. Your conscious mind became focused on something so that your subconscious could take over. The hypnosis might not have been deep, and you may have come in and out of it several times, but the basic principle is the same as if you were on a stage or in a therapist's office.

It's important to recognize this detail because you occasionally run into people who are afraid of hypnosis. They think that by going into a trance, they will lose control of themselves with their own thoughts. That's not the way hypnotism works. You can bring yourself out of a trance at any time, and you won't do anything that puts yourself into danger.

Consider this: when you go to sleep at night, you may toss and turn all over your bed. But even though you aren't conscious while you're sleeping, you are very, very unlikely to fall onto the floor no matter how much you move. That's a good analogy for the way hypnotism works. Even though you might not be conscious in the traditional sense that you are used to while under a trance, you aren't under the complete control of another person either. Instead, you're simply receiving suggestions on a deeper level.

Hypnosis Can be Induced or Created in Several Ways

Most hypnotists will have their favorite ways of creating a hypnotic state, but the reality is that there are dozens or hundreds of different ways to bring a subject into a trance. As I mentioned already, it can even happen by accident without someone realizing it!

Within the hypnotic community, we call the different methods of pulling someone into a hypnotic trance "inductions." That's because a good hypnotist *induces* someone's mind into a state of relaxation using proven techniques that revert the brain back to a focused state. Remember: we aren't controlling people, just helping them to reach a level of clarity that they can already move to naturally. Then we deepen it a bit so they can become more receptive to the ideas coming their way.

Hypnotic inductions come in many different varieties. One popular technique is to progressively relax a subject, bringing their awareness to different parts of the body and having them let all tension slip away. Doing so gives the subject a chance to focus their mind on one thought at a time, clearing away other conscious distractions. With a little bit of effort and calming, they can open themselves to new suggestions that aren't sidetracked by the normal mental chatter we are also accustomed to listening to.

Relaxing hypnotic inductions are popular because they tend to be very effective, even with people who haven't been hypnotized before. However, the downside (especially for a stage hypnotist who needs to keep a comedy show moving along) is that they take a while. In their place, some hypnotists will use specific visualizations that force subjects to concentrate intensely. These have the similar effect of getting participants to tune out the world around them and open their subconscious minds to suggestion.

Some stage hypnotists and street performers will even use what are called "rapid" or "instant" hypnotic inductions. These may take seconds instead of minutes, and work by triggering the subconscious mind through distraction, disruption, and visual cues. The fact that they work so quickly adds to the drama and entertainment value of the situation.

In the end, each style of hypnotic induction does the same thing: it pulls the subject into a state of focus and relaxation. In a couple of chapters, I'm going to show you how you can use a reliable technique to frame and absorb your own suggestions. You'll see for yourself that hypnosis is completely natural, and that it is incredibly easy to slip into a hypnotic state once you're used to it.

In Hypnosis, Your Mind Becomes More Flexible

During a stage hypnosis show, a person will often behave strangely based on a suggestion. To go back to an early (and popular) example, you'll sometimes see hypnotic subjects cluck like chickens. Or in a therapist's office, they may be taken back to an earlier age at which something happened that set the stage for future habits and impressions.

To someone observing this, it can seem as if the subject is playing along. But to the person being hypnotized, the experience is absolutely real. They feel that they *are* a chicken in that moment, and really *are* being taken back to moments from their childhood. It's not hard to explain: once you take conscious thought out of the equation, the mind becomes incredibly flexible.

There is a very easy way to analogize this for skeptics. Think back to the last time you watched a really sad movie. Maybe there was an instant where a character had to say goodbye to a loved one, or a favorite pet passed away. Such a storyline is bound to bring a number of viewers to tears, and to incite feelings of sadness and loss in just about everyone who watches. This is true even though everyone who sees the movie knows that what's happening isn't true. They are aware that the people in the movie are actors are reading lines, that special effects are being used, and that scripts are being followed. The emotions are real, even if the situation isn't.

If someone yawns next to you, you might do so as well out of the sheer force of habit. Laughter and excitement spread in groups, too, as you can see in any comedy club or political rally. The fatigue, joy, or determination that accompanies these events are all genuine, even if the inspiration has been drawn from elsewhere.

In a focused or hypnotic state, your mind is extraordinarily flexible. It can adopt new habits or beliefs readily, acting upon them with no effort. This allows you to set new goals, shed old fears, and see yourself differently more quickly than you might expect. Once you get past the entertainment value of hypnotism, this ability to create change can lead to truly amazing outcomes.

Changing Your Mind Changes Your Life

It's crucial to keep in mind that we all tend to act in accordance with our subconscious beliefs. Whatever we've accepted deeply in our own minds will be reflected in our attitudes and behaviors going forward. It's also handy to remember that most of us didn't pick these impressions consciously. Instead, they were fed to us through our parents, friends, teachers, and even the media.

Often, the most happy and successful people you'll ever meet are the ones who have taken control of their subconscious selves and started to draw their own mental pictures. Then, they can live in a way that makes them feel good and brings them towards their most important goals.

When you change what your mind believes on a subconscious level, you change every aspect of your attitude. You literally see the world and yourself in a different way. Your inner brain can make you cluck like a chicken, but it can also lead you to soar like an eagle. It's all a matter of what you really think when your conscious thoughts are stripped away.

CHAPTER FOUR:

HYPNOSIS IN ACTION

ONCE I can convince someone who is skeptical that hypnosis is in fact real, the next thing they almost always want to know is how they can put it to good use. In my experience, the possibilities are nearly endless. There aren't many parts of your life that *can't* be improved with focused hypnotic practice. Things like health, wealth, positivity, and relationships are all functions of attitude. Change your thinking about them, and you'll get new outcomes.

In a more practical sense, however, therapists and individuals tend to use hypnosis in a handful of settings again and again. I could certainly make the case that altering the mind is the perfect solution to these particular issues, and that's a point of view I absolutely agree with. However, it's also true that these tend to be the challenges people struggle with most often.

To look at it another way, almost any challenge in your life gets easier to overcome when you attack it at a subconscious level. So, I don't want you to feel constrained by the list I'm about to give you – if you want to work on something I don't suggest, feel free to experiment with self-hypnosis or consult a professional. On the other hand, if the change you want to create in your life happens to coincide with the changes 95% of the population is also trying to deal with, then know that you're on the right track.

With that being said, let's first look at some common issues that can be dealt with hypnotically. Then, we'll wrap this chapter up with a few reasons hypnosis is a better answer to these issues than most other kinds of treatment and therapy that might be available to you.

Let's begin by looking at some of the most popular reasons people decide to try hypnosis for behavioral change.

Smoking and Addiction

Tobacco users tend to focus on the chemical aspects of their addictions. However, these usually represent only a small part of the habit. The real reason people can't quit smoking has to do with other factors, like the fact that it makes them feel less stressed. Or perhaps because someone they admire used to smoke, or they like the social aspects. Change the mental associations they have with nicotine (or any other addiction), and the behavior will follow suit. They don't "quit smoking," they just start to feel like non-smokers. You could substitute almost any other addiction for nicotine and get the same results.

Weight Loss

A similar dynamic often plays out when it comes to health and weight loss. Making the decision to eat healthier foods and get more exercise is easy, but following through isn't. The subconscious likes what is known, familiar, and comforting. Plus, if someone believes deep down that they should be overweight, that mental picture has to be changed before any weight loss can become permanent. That's why hypnosis can be so much more effective than your typical diet.

Stress and Anxiety

Most of us live high-stress lives. We are constantly being bombarded with choices and deadlines at work, and don't necessarily practice healthy and relaxing habits at home. Over time, this can make us feel chronically tired, irritated, and less productive or creative than we should be. One of the beautiful side effects of hypnosis is that it's incredibly relaxing. Some subjects say they feel better after spending a half hour in a trance then they do after eight hours of sleep. Whether it's specifically for stress relief or as part of a bigger behavior modification program, hypnosis can be a wonderful tool for winding down.

Fears and Phobias

Fears and phobias come in many different forms. In each case, though, they can hold us back from doing something special. For instance, the person who is afraid of flying may (consciously or subconsciously) avoid a promotion that involves more travel. Or a person could miss out on a lifelong dream to go scuba diving because they have an irrational fear of sharks. Once again, changing the mental side of things is the quickest way to create a breakthrough. Once that happens, it's not a matter of living with a fear or getting past it; instead, it's as if the phobia was never there in the first place.

Confidence and Self-Esteem

Different aspects of our self-esteem are formed when we are very young and at transformational points in our lives. Unfortunately, the inputs and messages we receive from loved ones and the world at large aren't always positive. They can leave us with a lack of self-worth that isn't in line with our talents and abilities. Using hypnosis, we can begin to see ourselves in a different way, emphasizing our best qualities and overcoming any insecurities that might have been holding us back. When we start to see ourselves as winners, others pick up the same point of view. That makes hypnosis for confidence and self-esteem relevant to every part of our lives.

Sports Performance

Professionals and amateurs alike know that competition is all about getting a mental edge. If you can't step onto a court or field with the proper mindset, you've lost before the game has even been played. You can use hypnosis to mentally rehearse different activities, calm jittery nerves, and think of yourself as a top performer in any game or athletic competition. Adjusting your perspective in this way helps you not only to bring out the best in yourself, but to enjoy your favorite sports even more.

Career Goals

You can absolutely use hypnosis to earn a promotion, get ahead in your field, and make more money. Whether you want to sell more to clients, give better presentations, or simply adjust your habits in the office, changing your mindset is the first step. You can even use the power of hypnosis to alter the feelings you have about your job and career, allowing you to focus on the positive and meaningful aspects. Once you do, you may find that you spring out of bed a little faster, bring a better attitude to your job, and make a stronger impression on your colleagues and supervisors.

I'd like to stress once again that this is *not* an exhaustive list of the changes that can be created with hypnosis. It's really up to you to explore your own goals and imagination when it comes to adjusting your own mindset. By thinking about yourself and the challenges you face differently, you open up a whole new range of possibilities that wasn't there before.

Why Use Hypnosis?

Having brought up some of the things you can change with hypnosis, it's worth exploring why you would want to approach any of these challenges through your subconscious. After all, there are numerous products and services in place to help already. From nicotine patches to diet plans and anxiety pills, there are a lot of places you could look for assistance. Why focus on hypnotism?

As it turns out, there are a lot of reasons to change your mind instead of looking for more drastic solutions.

For one thing, hypnosis is incredibly cost effective. Booking a session with a hypnotherapist won't take a big bite out of your wallet, and as you'll see very shortly, you can even save on those expenses by hypnotizing yourself. Why spend money you don't have to when a better answer is available?

Another huge benefit of hypnosis is that it can work quickly. I've seen smokers who were going through two packs a day quit after an hour of therapy. The moment they stop seeing themselves as nicotine users, the habit no longer feels natural. They don't want to buy cigarettes, or even be around them, so their behavior follows suit and it's like they never had the craving in the first place.

That brings me to another benefit, which is that hypnotism can often solve problems that can't be fixed in other ways. Nicotine patches, for instance, or anti-anxiety medications just push symptoms to the back of the mind. Using hypnosis, you can attack the underlying issue itself. That's why working with your subconscious tends to yield better long-term results than special diets, patches, or medications do.

Unlike a lot of treatments, hypnosis doesn't come with any harmful side effects. In fact, you'll leave each session feeling better than when you started. You may begin to notice that you are more calm and focused in every area of your life, and that your sleep improves. That's not exactly what you would get from your average shot or pill.

Finally, hypnosis is a completely natural state. The more you slip into a hypnotic trance, the deeper you go and the better you get at it. That means you can develop the ability to set the course for your subconscious more acutely over time. You'll find it's easier and easier to improve your own life. You might start out using hypnotism for smoking or weight loss, for example, but take what you've learned to do a better job at work and earn more money.

The question, really, isn't why you would use hypnosis to solve your problems. Instead, it's just a matter of figuring out which goals are most important to you now so that you can get to work on your subconscious mind.

CHAPTER FIVE:

HOW TO HYPNOTIZE YOURSELF

IF you've been following me up to this point, you'll know that hypnosis is a completely natural state. There isn't anything mystical about it; it's just a matter of focusing your mind and relaxing your body so you can take in new suggestions.

For those who are new to hypnosis, it can be helpful to work with a professional therapist who can pull you into a hypnotic state and let you experience the sensation in a safe and guided environment. However, there isn't anything wrong with learning to do this on your own. After all, hypnotism is like anything in life: it just takes a little bit of practice. If you devote a bit of time to it every day, you'll be pulling yourself into a peaceful, productive trance in no time at all.

With that being said, there is an in between option. There are numerous recordings you can use that will allow you to become hypnotized in the privacy of your own home (check out my website for some programs that focus on specific goals). You could also choose to create your own recordings using the techniques I outline below. This might require a little more time and effort, but would allow you to customize your suggestions perfectly for your goal or situation.

As you'll see, it's not difficult to hypnotize yourself quickly and easily.

Begin Self-Hypnosis With the Right Setting

With a few exceptions, you'll notice that most hypnotists like to work in a quiet, relaxed setting. Even if it's in the middle of a comedy show on a stage, they'll typically ask the audience to remain silent during a hypnotic induction. That's not to say that you need ideal settings to create a hypnotic trance – some performers work on busy streets with no problems. But, by giving yourself the right setting, you're likely to be more comfortable, pull yourself into a hypnotic trance more quickly, and go deeper into your subconscious then you would if you were continually being interrupted.

With that in mind, try to choose the right environment for your relaxing hypnotic experience. Choose a comfortable place in a quiet room where you are unlikely to be disturbed. If possible, go into hypnosis at a time when you feel relaxed and aren't too tired. You may want to experiment with a few different options, or even undergo hypnosis two or three times throughout your day. Practice makes perfect, and the benefits only get better with time.

It can also be prudent to set a timer or alarm that will signal the end of your hypnosis session if you go too long (just don't use one with a jarring tone at the end!). Although hypnosis is a state of focused relaxation rather than sleep, it's not unheard of for someone to drift off into slumber during the session, particularly if they were already fatigued. Having a reminder you can hear will ensure that you won't lose track of time, and will put your mind at ease so you don't have to worry about that happening.

It goes without saying that you should *never* attempt hypnosis while you're doing something that requires your attention. Don't listen to hypnotic recordings in cars, while operating machinery, using knives to make dinner, etc.

Your Self-Hypnosis Induction

You may remember from an earlier chapter that hypnotists use inductions to help subjects relax and bring them into a deeper state of trance. That's exactly what I'm going to ask you to do with yourself. The process you will use is one of progressive relaxation that has been used again and again in millions of situations. It is relatively quick, and very effective.

Note once again that you may find it easier to relax and follow the steps if you use the aid of a recording. If you do, I encourage you to read the following into a microphone using a calm voice:

Begin by placing your feet flat on the floor and setting your hands beside you a comfortable position.

Choose a spot or object on a nearby wall and focus your attention on it completely. Try to leave your eyes fixed on that point as you breathe deeply in and out. You may notice that after some time your vision will become slightly blurry and your eyes will strain. Continue to breathe in and out slowly and deeply. When your eyes began to feel heavy, go ahead and close them.

Next, take a series of even deeper, slower breaths in and out. Relax, knowing that this time is for you and the goal you have created for yourself. That's it. Breathe in deeply, hold it for just a moment, and then let it release.

Do the same again a few more times. As you breathe in, think the word "sleep." And as you exhale, imagine the words "deep sleep" coming out of your mouth and then dissipating away into the room around you.

With your eyes closed and your mind remaining still, continue breathing deeply while you mentally count down from ten. With that first number, feel a sense of warmth and relaxation descending onto your head from above. Let all the tiny muscles in your eyelids go completely limp. Relax your jaw. Let your tongue hang heavily in your mouth.

Now count down to nine and let all of the tension release from your neck. Fall back into your chair or couch more deeply if it feels comfortable.

Continue to breathe deeply as you move to the number eight and feel every ounce of rigidity slip away from your shoulders. Let them fall loose and limp as you keep breathing deeply.

Upon reaching the number seven, let your back and spine go loose. Let go of any stiffness and sink down even further.

Six. Let your stomach and abdomen be limp. Feel that sense of warmth and looseness moving down your body one inch at a time.

At five, allow your hips and buttocks to lose any tension as well. Imagine yourself being rooted to the spot where you are sitting. You could rise if you wanted to, but every shred of rigidity is gone. Instead, there is only total relaxation.

Four. Feel the muscles of your upper legs and thighs lose all of their stiffness. Know that you are sinking deeper into relaxation as you breathe ever more deeply and slowly.

Now that you've reached three, allow your knees to be loose and limp. Don't hold onto any tension.

At two, let your calves and lower leg muscles drain themselves of all strength. Feel only warmth and relaxation.

Finally, all the way down to one, relax every tiny muscle and joint in your feet. Feel them being rooted to the floor like slabs of stone. Enjoy the sensation of being in a state of utter stillness, and imagine that you are sliding deeper and deeper into a sense of peace now.

Giving Yourself Hypnotic Suggestions

When you have followed this induction and find yourself in a completely relaxed state, it's time to begin sending messages to your subconscious mind. The beautiful thing about this process is that you can absorb new ideas and attitudes without giving up the sense of peace and warmth you've gained at this point. In other words, your body and mind are going on vacation while your subconscious sets you on a new path.

Because there is both an art and a science to creating hypnotic suggestions, I'm going to tackle the job of writing them in the next chapter. For now, just know that this is the point where your mind is ready to absorb something new. Deciding which direction to steer it in is entirely your choice.

Also note that the first few times you try this, you may want to simply hypnotize yourself to see how it feels. Once you can experience the calm and relaxed sensation in an easy way, you can always add or adjust your suggestions as needed.

Coming Out of Hypnosis

After you have followed your induction and given yourself some productive suggestions, it's time to end your self-hypnosis session. The best way to do this – and the way that will leave you feeling the most refreshed – is to follow the process gradually in reverse.

What I like to do is count upward from 1 to 5, slowly, adjusting from a hypnotic trance to a normal waking state. You could end your recording with something like the following:

Now it's time to bring your awareness back to the present and your surroundings.

One, feeling a sense of movement return to the feet and legs.

Two, letting that awareness come back to the back and midsection.

Three, rolling the shoulders, the head, and the neck slightly.

Four, becoming aware of the sounds around me and reorienting myself in my chair and my room.

Five, letting the eyes open with the sensation of being completely refreshed and renewed, ready to take on any new goal or challenge.

And with that, you're fully awake and better than ever!

Hypnosis is a Habit

Remember that hypnosis is a habit and a skill. The more you practice it, the better you'll get. If you find in the beginning that you have a hard time calming your mind, that you shift in your chair uncomfortably while you're listening to your induction, or can't fully focus, that's all right. Most of us live stressful lives in which we are used to dealing with constant distractions. Keep at it, though, and you'll find yourself going into a trance more deeply and quickly than you would have imagined.

At that point, it's simply a matter of giving your subconscious mind the right instructions to follow. Let's move on to the next chapter to see exactly how that's done.

CHAPTER SIX:

YOUR SCRIPT FOR POSITIVE CHANGE

WITH a little bit of practice, it's easy to put yourself into a relaxed hypnotic state. What you do once you're there can have big effects on the rest of your life. While many people enjoy hypnosis simply for the fact that it's such a great way to calm down and relieve stress, you will probably be at least somewhat curious to find out what you could accomplish by altering your subconscious thought patterns.

Professional hypnotists sometimes refer to hypnotic trance as a "resource state." That's because it allows us to work with our subjects or clients on a level that would be impossible during normal, day-to-day conversation. We can help to instill or reinforce ideas, impressions, and emotions that would otherwise take years to put in place.

However, there are a few rules of the road for dealing with the subconscious mind. Tone, phrasing, and intention become very important.

You don't just have to choose the right ideas; you also have to construct them in a way that makes sense on a deep mental level. For that reason, a lot of hypnotists – and particularly hypnotherapists – will work from a set of scripts that can be tailored or customized to a particular client's needs. These can be used as a roadmap of suggestions that takes a person from where they are now to a different behavior or attitude in the future.

Additionally, using hypnotic scripts means professionals don't have to "reinvent the wheel" every time they put a subject into trance. They already have a set of ideas they know will work.

In this chapter, I'm going to share with you the basics of a good hypnotic suggestion. Then, I'm going to give you a handful of examples you can adapt for use in your own life. By combining these with the self-hypnosis formula given in the last chapter, you'll have everything you need to first change your mind, and then change your life.

Keep Hypnotic Suggestions Positive

When hypnotizing yourself, you should stick to suggestions that are positive in nature. Frame them in terms of what you are moving toward, rather than anything you want to stop or avoid.

There are couple of reasons your hypnotic suggestions need to be positive. The first has to do with a simple aspect of motivation: we are more likely to be driven over the long term by focusing on what we want instead of worrying about what we can't have. All of us want to be healthy, fit, and attractive. But, few of us relish the thought of giving up cigarettes or our favorite junk foods. If we only pay attention to the things we are used to having or are currently missing out on, the temptation to indulge in them becomes stronger. By keeping our attention on a positive goal, though, we can maintain a better frame of mind.

In a more structural sense, you should know that our subconscious minds take things literally and struggle with negative statements. If you say to yourself "I will not eat donuts" during a trance state, your inner brain may ignore the negative part of that statement and absorb the opposite message from the one you're looking for.

For both of these reasons, every hypnotic suggestion you give yourself should be framed in a positive way. Move toward your dreams rather than train your mind to focus its attention on what you can't have.

Hypnotic Suggestions Need to Be Very Specific

As I mentioned just a moment ago, your subconscious mind is incredibly literal. It doesn't detect nuance, irony, or generalities. It's much, much better to tell yourself that you are "running 5 miles per day" than that you are "getting healthier." One is concrete and easy to define. The other is vague and almost impossible to pin down.

Whatever suggestions you are going to provide to your own mind, they have to be measurable. Aim for things that are tangible enough to know whether you are on track to accomplish them, and that you'll know when you have. Otherwise, your subconscious may become confused by the suggestions and ignore them altogether.

One big benefit of this approach is that it forces you to be more careful when thinking about the kind of change you want to affect in your life. It's easy to simply wish for things and hope they will happen. It takes more effort to actually reach inside yourself to decide what it is you hope to accomplish and express it in terms of numbers, figures, or hard results.

The more clearly you can define your thinking, the easier it will be to create and reach a goal that matters to you. This also happens to be a necessity when it comes to writing hypnotic suggestions and having your subconscious mind accept them.

Frame Your Hypnotic Suggestions in the Present Tense

Because your subconscious mind is so literal, it tends to not worry too much about the past or future. That's why you can be so easily swayed to give into the craving for that slice of pizza now, even though you might feel bad about it tomorrow. Your inner brain wants comfort at this moment, and it isn't concerned about the consequences that may arise later.

Knowing that, you should frame the change you want to make in your life as if you had already achieved it. For instance, telling yourself "I weigh 150 pounds" creates a concrete image in your subconscious. Writing your script "I *will* weigh 150 pounds in the future" creates uncertainty and is less actionable. The deeper parts of your mind are going to act in accordance with the image you hold of yourself. Believe that you are your ideal weight, and your lifestyle will adapt to correspond with that belief. Tell yourself that you'll meet a goal in the future, and you might find that the future you have envisioned with your conscious mind never really arrives.

This goes along with the standard piece of advice to "fake it until you make it." Your job under hypnosis is to change your mental perception of yourself and your life in a positive way. Simply keep affirming during your self-hypnosis sessions that you are what you want to be and your brain will keep finding ways to make your new affirmations a reality.

Hypnotic Suggestions Need to be Emotional

I've saved the most important detail of self-hypnotic suggestions for last. Your subconscious is swayed by feelings, not facts and statistics. When you're trying to change your own mind or perception, appeal to your own emotions. Focus on whatever it is that makes you excited and radiant.

When writing your suggestions out beforehand (and you definitely *should* write them out), use words like *excited* and *energized*. These help reinforce existing emotions, but also give another element of positivity to every suggestion. They activate the deeper parts of your brain and inspire you on a deeper level.

Consider for a moment two possible scenarios: in the first, I offer you a 3% monthly raise on your current income for working an extra hour a week. In the second, I tell you that if you show up earlier on Monday morning I'll hand you a suitcase stuffed with cash. Both of these situations point to the same basic outcome. Only one gets your heart rate moving, though. That's why subconscious suggestions need to be emotional.

Also, it's important to not only frame your suggestions in an emotional way, but to choose goals that make you feel excited in the first place. If you choose to focus on a goal in your self-hypnosis sessions just because you think you should, or to please someone else, it's not going to have much power in your mind.

A Few Examples of Hypnotic Suggestions

Putting these points together, we can come up with a handful of simple hypnotic suggestions you can use in your own life:

- "I am earning $100,000 per year as an executive in my company."
- "Running 5 miles every morning makes me feel fit, energized, and stress-free."
- "I love being a non-smoker who can keep up with my grandchildren."
- "My business is creating $1,000 of passive income every week."
- "I weigh 150 pounds, and love the way eating a vegetarian diet fills me with energy and positivity."

These are just simple examples, of course, and might not fit the goals you are trying to reach. However, they give you a set of templates that you can adapt and use in your own life. They also show how easy it is to create positive, specific, and emotionally-engaging suggestions that you can use to reprogram your mind in any way you would like.

Plugging in Your Hypnotic Suggestions

Making use of your hypnotic suggestions is incredibly easy. When making a recording to guide yourself through the process of self-hypnosis as described in the last chapter, simply repeat the statement you need to hear a dozen times or so. That way, it will only take you a few minutes to get into and out of trance, and your most important goal will be reinforced again and again.

I want to make two quick points before we wrap this chapter up, however. The first is that you should focus on one major goal at a time. You can certainly write different statements that surround that goal and build on one another, but be sure to concentrate on one big change in your life before moving on to another. Your subconscious can only focus on so many things at once, so choose whatever matters most to you right now.

The second thing I want to mention, once again, is that hypnosis is all about practice and repetition. Although a small percentage of individuals can take a hypnotic suggestion and permanently change their subconscious right away, most of us will require a few weeks (or even months) before something new will sink in. You've had your whole life to build up the habits and thought patterns that fill your mind now. Don't be surprised if it takes a little bit of time to nudge your inner mind in a new direction.

CHAPTER SEVEN:

OTHER WAYS TO REINFORCE YOUR HAPPY HABITS

It is my firm belief that most people, using two or three brief self-hypnosis sessions a day, can change their lives in just a few months. They can adopt new habits and attitudes that seem almost unimaginable to them now, and break through any resistance they've felt to change in the past.

It is impossible for me to overstate the importance of the subconscious mind, and the value of self-belief when it comes to reaching a goal. But that doesn't mean that self-hypnosis is the only way to create change or that you should rely strictly on your own hypnotic suggestions to find and achieve what is most important to you.

While much of the public tends to think of hypnotism as a gimmick, a party trick, or a mystical art, what it *really* amounts to is basic psychology applied in an interesting way. As hypnotists we learn a lot about the mind and the way it works. That gives us a bit of perspective on other tools and tricks you can use to change your habits and become a happier, healthier person.

With that in mind, I want to devote this short chapter to a few techniques you can use to reinforce your happy habits and make the most of the hypnotic suggestions you are feeding your mind on a daily basis. Here are a few I definitely want you to try...

Don't Give Yourself an Impossible Task

While it's true that your subconscious mind dictates much of your behavior and beliefs, and that your thought patterns can be changed quickly, personal transformation is easier when it's taken in steps. In other words, don't decide to suddenly turn your whole life upside down in pursuit of a goal that seems so unrealistic that you have almost no chance of success.

I give this advice not because I don't want you to make the most of every day, but because experience has shown me that new habits and attitudes are easier to implement in stages. The person who is used to eating donuts and pizza doesn't turn into a marathon runner overnight. Instead, they began by jogging a few miles each morning, establish a baseline of fitness with better eating, and then move on to bigger and better things.

These kinds of transitions are less taxing on the subconscious mind. Remember, your inner brain wants to keep you safe by holding onto existing habits. Gradual improvement is also easier to handle physically, financially, and in an everyday sense. The less you turn your life upside down, the easier it is to remain calm and keep your eyes on the big picture.

Use the Power of Visuals for Motivation

You can use self-hypnosis to retrain your subconscious thought patterns and stay focused on a goal. In between those sessions, however, you can remind yourself of what you're working for by putting the power of visual cues to use.

If you are at all active on social media, then you have undoubtedly noticed that pictures and videos tend to stand out more than other types of content (especially text). That's because our minds are configured to grab onto images quickly, and to process them emotionally. Long ago, our ancestors had to identify threats and prey in an instant. They saw things and interpreted the information long before they knew how to read. Our world has evolved since then, but the oldest parts of our brain haven't.

When you have a picture of your dream house, a photo of the car you want to buy, or some other visual reminder that's always in or near your field of vision, your mind is going to focus on it. You'll continually be reminded of what you're working towards, which can help you stay motivated and "locked in" when you're trying to reach your goal.

As you turn your attention towards creating a specific target for your mind to focus on, see if you can find a few pictures that remind you of it continually. These will reinforce the hypnotic suggestions you've been accepting in your mind, and can keep you from becoming distracted.

Reward Yourself for Good Habits

Going back to Pavlov and other early psychologists, it has been well-established that living organisms of any kind (humans included) will tend to seek out pleasure and avoid pain. The stronger the pleasure and the sharper the pain, the more you will associate a habit with the immediate feedback.

For an easy example, we can go back to eating habits. When you consume a piece of chocolate, you get an immediate sense of gratification. The taste and texture serve as a "reward" for eating it. Imagine that you could tie that feeling to a different habit you want to reinforce. For example, suppose that for each day you accomplished a goal at work, you were rewarded with a small treat of some kind. It wouldn't take long before you would subconsciously begin to push yourself to succeed at the office. Consciously, you know that your improved performance is likely to lead to a big bonus or other career benefits. Subconsciously, though, your inner brain will keep you moving because it wants that piece of chocolate.

You could take this the other way, as well. Every workday that you *didn't* do what you needed to, you could give yourself a punishment. Faced with the prospect of either getting a piece of chocolate or having to spend half an hour on filing, for instance, your subconscious will seek out the reward rather than the rebuke. That means if you have the discipline to be honest with yourself, you can reinforce your hypnotic suggestions consistently by awarding rewards and punishments based on your behavior.

This is a very simple way to modify your habits, but it works. What kind of treat could you use to encourage a new habit, and what would you be willing to take away if you were to fall short of reaching it?

Share Your Progress With Others

As people, we tend to discount the effect that social influences have on our lives. We all think we do things for our own reasons, ignoring the fact that the people around us can affect our behavior in big ways.

There are so many psychological studies proving this point that it would be useless to mention them. All of us are susceptible to group thinking on some level, and we definitely care about the perceptions and impressions that surround us. This isn't a good thing or a bad thing; it's just human nature. It's how we use it that matters most.

If you accept that we are all swayed by the thoughts and opinions of others, then why not use peer pressure to back up your self-hypnosis efforts? You could join a group that's devoted to fitness, business networking, or some other personal achievement. The other members will encourage great habits and offer positive and encouraging feedback. That social interaction can become addictive, reinforcing good habits all on its own.

Working towards your goals in the full view of others also creates a sense of accountability. We don't want to be diminished in the eyes of our friends and family or let them down, so we work harder to achieve the things we have said we were going to. Besides, the victories we achieve are all the better when we have others to share them with.

Repetition is a Powerful Force

In my mind, there isn't any question that hypnosis is the most powerful, versatile, and useful tool for changing thoughts and behavior. You can literally think yourself happy if you follow the proven formulas I've laid out in this book.

However, just because something works on some level doesn't mean you need to use it as your only channel for motivation and change. Visualization, rewards and punishments, and social pressure all contribute to self-improvement. Knowing that, why wouldn't you use them to influence your own mind and habits? If nothing else, they'll make the changes you are implementing through hypnosis take hold faster and become more deeply ingrained. It only makes sense to use all the tools at your disposal when you're trying to do something important.

What I'm really getting to here is the power of repetition. Our minds tend to hold onto big events, but in reality it's usually the little things that end up making the big difference. An earthquake can shift the landscape for a few miles, but it took rivers and glaciers millions of years to form the Grand Canyon. Hypnosis can implant an idea in your mind, but lots of subtle psychological reminders make any change or transition easier and smoother.

Just by reading this book, you are probably closer than you've ever been to reaching your most important goals. Use the tips I've outlined in this chapter to pull out all the stops when it comes to making them a reality.

CHAPTER EIGHT:

BUILDING YOURSELF UP FROM THE INSIDE OUT

As powerful as hypnosis and behavior modification techniques are when it comes to reaching your goals, there is another aspect to personal change that shouldn't be overlooked. Namely, it has to do with the way you communicate with yourself.

For whatever reason, a lot of us are learning to be our own worst critics at an early age. It could be that we compare ourselves to others who seem to be more talented and driven. Or perhaps we associate with family members who put us (or themselves) down on a regular basis. Whatever the cause, millions upon millions of adults are walking around each day minimizing their own good qualities and mentally exaggerating the characteristics that they aren't so proud of.

How often do you find yourself saying that you can't do something, that you don't have what others do, or that the success you want isn't achievable? Now ask yourself the second question: how could those ideas *not* be absorbed by your subconscious mind?

Psychological researchers have proven that you can put yourself in a better mood simply by forcing your face to smile. That is, you don't have to feel a genuine grin when you do it – just going through the act will make you feel better.

By the same token, learning to look at your life in a different way can actually affect your outlook and improve your capacity for change. Once you feel like a stronger, more confident individual, you'll start to act like one. Then, you'll feel like you can take on anything, including your most important goals.

So how do you build yourself up from the inside out? It's surprisingly easy. Here are a few techniques you can use to get started...

Learn to Speak a New Language

As I've mentioned, both positive and negative language are almost hypnotic in their effect on the subconscious. The more you say something, the more you start to believe it. So it's crucial that you only say things you want to actually accept.

One simple improvement you can make right now is to eliminate negative statements from your vocabulary. Break the habit of using phrases like

"I can't." Stop telling yourself, and others, that you aren't strong enough, smart enough, good-looking enough, or enough of anything else to get the happiness you deserve.

Of course, speech patterns are habits, meaning they can be difficult to break. A good first step in this direction is to use positive self-hypnosis suggestions, as I suggested earlier in the book. Another way is to make yourself aware of the language you are using through physical reminders.

For example, one technique that works particularly well is to tie a rubber band around your wrist. Every time you use phrases like "I can't," you snap yourself with the rubber band. In that instant, you will get a quick and immediate reminder that you reverted back to old ways. For extra effectiveness, you could even get others to help you. They can snap your rubber band, or remind you to do so whenever you stray off-script.

You would be amazed at how quickly you can use this technique to change your habit of speaking. You'll be even more amazed at how differently you start to feel when you speak like someone who can do anything.

Embrace Positive Affirmations

The idea of using positive affirmations to build up self-esteem isn't a new one. It's an idea that dates all the way back to philosophers in the Middle Ages. While many parts of life have changed since then, the basic physiology of the human brain hasn't.

Recall what I wrote just a few paragraphs back. Simply changing your facial expression will alter your mood in a matter of 10 to 15 seconds or less. You can make that effect stronger by combining it with a written or spoken statement. The more you see and repeat something, the more likely you are to not only believe it but to internalize it.

In the same way that you created positive hypnotic suggestions, you could write out a set of three to five uplifting affirmations that tell you you're a good person, a talented individual, a smart negotiator, a great salesperson, or a fit, athletic, and attractive adult. Then, you could read these to yourself for a few minutes each morning and evening in the mirror until they start to feel true. Do it with the right facial expressions and tone of voice, and they'll sink in even faster.

You have more control over the way you see yourself than you might imagine. Write down what it is you need to know or believe, and then ride those affirmations to a healthier perspective and a happier point of view.

Take Your Weaknesses Head On

There is a big difference between emphasizing your best qualities and outright lying to yourself. When changing your self-talk or building affirmations, you should prioritize things you're proud of, or aspirations that you have. That's a way to bring out the best in yourself. Another way is to minimize or overcome any challenges you might be facing, especially since these are probably going to be mental roadblocks. In other words, you shouldn't be afraid to tackle your weaknesses head on.

Most of us already know where our biggest challenges and unfortunate tendencies lie. Perhaps we aren't as focused as we should be, tend to give up on things too easily, or compare ourselves with others more than we should. Those are all completely normal and natural human traits. And, they all get easier to counteract once we are actually aware of them.

Just acknowledging a problem and being honest with yourself about it can change the way you feel. Denial is never helpful, but bringing an issue into the light takes some of its strength away. Moreover, it gives you a chance to think about what the challenge is keeping you from, and ways you might confront it.

So, either brainstorm in the third person or talk to some people who are closest to you who might be willing to be honest. Ask them what's preventing you from having the success you're hoping for. Be willing to listen both to your own mind and others without being defensive.

Once you have the answers, start looking for resources you can use to deal with the problem. These might include books, seminars, or trained professionals. Whatever you need, don't just shy away and hope you find it. It can be tough to confront our own weaknesses, but getting past them is a good way to build up self-esteem and break out of old patterns.

Create a Positive Social Circle

Earlier in this book, I advised you to seek out like-minded people who can help you to stay accountable and focused on whatever it is you're trying to achieve. You might apply that same sort of thinking to your social circle, as well.

We all have friends and family members who build us up, and we've all known others whose first inclination is to tear us down. Why waste time or emotional energy on the people who aren't going to support us or help us to live our dreams? Where is the benefit in that?

You can love someone without spending a lot of time with them, and it's perfectly acceptable to prioritize your own happiness over old relationships or obligations if there is an individual in your life who doesn't make you feel all that great about yourself. Luckily, though, things rarely get to that point. If you have a colleague or loved one who doesn't seem to be a positive influence, simply letting them know how you feel could change their behavior. Make them acknowledge that they aren't supporting you in your journey towards improvement, and that awareness might shift their perspective.

You have more control over your social circle, and the emotional messages you receive, then you might imagine. Make the most of that fact by surrounding yourself with people who see the very best in you and want you to feel great as a result.

Work With Professionals

In extreme cases, you may have difficultly changing your own self-image. As with any subconscious belief, the picture you hold of your own talents and abilities has been created over a lifetime of experience. You can't expect it to change in an instant.

Using the tips I've outlined, you can probably eliminate negative self-talk and build a stronger social network in just a few weeks. However, if you find that the challenge is overwhelming and you still feel less than “good enough” in some key area of your life, it might be time to turn to a professional for help.

Psychologists, therapists, coaches, mentors, and even hypnotherapists are all available to help you get the most from your life. If you feel embarrassed about searching for assistance, ask yourself what would be worse: reaching out to someone who has helped hundreds of thousands of others to deal with a specific problem, or living with it just because you are afraid of an uncomfortable conversation?

The better you feel about yourself, the easier it is to enjoy the benefits of self-hypnosis and turn a corner in your life. Are you seeing your best qualities as vividly as you should be?

CHAPTER NINE:

HYPNOTIZING YOURSELF FOR HAPPINESS

GIVEN that this short book is all about hypnotism and happiness, you might be wondering what I have left to say for this chapter on building a better life of mental strategies. That's fair – I've already walked you through the way the subconscious mind works, shown you how to reach it with the right sorts of suggestions, and even taught you what you can do to reinforce those ideas. What more could there be to add?

The answer isn't another technique, or even a new idea. Instead, it's a set of ideas and reminders that have come to me through years of experience working with subjects who were in a resource state. In other words, it's all the stuff I think you need to know to get the most from the information I've already given you that didn't fit in elsewhere. And I want to throw in a few words of encouragement.

With that out of the way, let me share a few things I think you should know about the process that's ahead of you...

Self-Hypnotism Really Works

I started this book by answering the one question I get more than any other: is hypnotism real? It absolutely is. But more importantly, hypnotizing yourself to change attitudes, beliefs, and behaviors *absolutely works*.

You make hundreds of small decisions every day based on what you believe about your own knowledge level, physical abilities, charisma, and so on. You have a vision of yourself, and an idea of where you fit in the world. If you change that vision in a noticeable way, then your behavior will adapt accordingly. You can go from being a smoker to a non-smoker almost instantly, for example, or begin to see yourself as someone who is fit, energetic, and able to achieve their goals.

People are amazed at what they see during hypnosis demonstrations because they underestimate the power of their own subconscious minds. If they only knew just how dramatically things can change with a true difference in perspective that starts with the inner brain, they would take on all kinds of new plans and projects with great confidence.

Don't fall into the trap of wondering whether self-hypnosis can really work for you. It absolutely can, and when it does you'll be able to achieve things you might not have thought possible in the past.

Your Goals and Focus May Shift Over Time

I have found that when most people realize how important subconscious change really is, they tend to have something in their life that they want to alter. Usually one priority stands out from all the others.

However, they may also have other secondary goals they want to achieve. Or, they might reach their first dream and wonder what to do next. They could even discover that what they want most shifts and changes over time. That's only natural. None of us can predict the future, and most of us can't even say with great confidence that we'll know which ideas we'll be chasing in a few months or years.

This brings us to the best thing about hypnosis for self-improvement. It works for almost *any* goal or situation, and you get better at it over time. So, while your immediate concern might be losing weight or giving up nicotine, the same process you're mastering right now can also be used to make more money, advance your career, or start your own business. It's a valuable way to improve your health, change your perspective or attitude, and even enhance your relationships with friends and loved ones.

By learning a few fundamentals of self-hypnosis, you are giving yourself the tools to affect virtually any kind of change you want to see in your life. The way you put those tools to use might differ over time, but the core skills are always going to be there.

Your Mind Likes to be Reminded of What's Important

Although hypnosis is in many ways more effective than any kind of medication or treatment, and can be used without danger or side effects, it tends to work differently for different people. Some men and women will respond to even big suggestions right away, making wholesome changes in their lives almost immediately. Every hypnotist knows someone who was pulled into a trance and gave up a bad habit (like smoking, alcohol, or overeating) in an hour or two. It happens.

For most of us, though, hypnosis – whether we're hypnotizing ourselves or working with others – takes a little bit of repetition. We can make the same kinds of changes in gains, but they might take a few sessions, or even a few weeks, instead of just one. And regardless of how long it takes to flip a mental switch, we can all be strengthened through regular reminders of what we're after.

The point I'm trying to make here is that you shouldn't expect hypnosis to fix your problem right away. It might, but I don't want you to count on it. And, no matter how talented you may or may not be as a hypnotic subject, know that each session is going to pull you deeper and have bigger subsequent effects. Influencing your subconscious is like working with compound interest; the more contributions you make, the bigger the payoffs are going to get.

You should not only try to find the time to use self-hypnosis once or twice a day, but you should also pay attention to the other psychological reinforcing techniques I outlined earlier in the book. Your subconscious likes to be reminded of what's important, and all the different tools work best in conjunction with one another.

What's Really Important to You?

Because your subconscious mind works on an emotional level, it is most responsive to the goals and ideas that feel exciting, invigorating, and even scary. It's challenged and activated by dreams that bring out your biggest and boldest emotions.

That makes the process of improvement through hypnosis an incredibly personal one. What truly drives you at a core level might not be all that important to someone else, or vice versa. Most people think that money, professional success, and other visible achievements are powerful incentives to change habits. Time and time again, however, I've seen that these are only drivers for a certain segment of the population. For others, time with family, intellectual puzzles, or even stability can be more valuable.

The point I want to make here is that you should be undergoing a process of continual self-exploration to determine what it is that really matters to you. Try to find the dreams that drag you out of bed in the morning, and make those the goals you set your sights upon. Don't worry about whether or not they seem applicable to others, or whether they even make sense to the people you know. What matters is that they inspire you, not that they be fun for you to talk about at a cocktail party.

This book is about happiness, not achievement, income, or status. For some of us, those might be the same things. But for everyone else, it's a matter of chasing a sense of joy and contentment.

Develop Momentum in Your Life

There is still a lot of ongoing debate about what hypnotism really is and how it works in the brain. Researchers have been able to prove that the hypnotic phenomenon is real, but they still disagree on why it is our minds have developed the ability to fall into a trance over the centuries.

My own point of view is that all of us have this mental resource state available to us because it's a necessity. There are times when we have to be hyper focused on threats and opportunities. We can use hypnosis to block out pain and distraction, or to fully comply with important instructions. It's a tool that can help us keep growing, learning, and improving in every aspect of our lives.

I have often observed that once someone realizes positive change is possible in one area, they'll translate that into others. The man who loses dozens of pounds and gets into shape suddenly finds he can take control of his career, too. The woman who conquers her bad habit or addiction decides to further her education at the same time. There's something addictive about getting the most from each day and breaking away from the constraints that seem to hold so many people back.

If you can master the art of hypnotizing yourself and using focused, positive suggestions to guide your mind in the right direction, then you can begin to create an unstoppable momentum in your personal and professional life. You suddenly feel like you have more control. Calm, peace, and happiness are easier to come by. And, of course, there's more fulfillment when you're getting closer to your dreams.

For me, hypnosis is all about happiness. Isn't it time to train your mind to seek out the things that are going to make you leap out of bed every morning ready to face a new day?

CHAPTER TEN:

10 FAQS ABOUT HYPNOTISM

BEFORE I bring this short book to a close, I wanted to devote a section to some of the most commonly asked questions I get about hypnosis. This isn't meant to be an all-inclusive informational guide, and many of the questions below have been answered in some way throughout the previous chapters.

Still, I've seen that after a hypnosis show or therapy session, people will inevitably ask a handful of things again and again. So, whether you've skipped ahead to find a piece of information, are simply curious about some aspect of hypnotism, or just want a few points to share with friends when you tell them about your self-hypnosis program, here are a few things you should know...

#1
How Long Has Hypnosis Been Around?

This is a somewhat misleading question. The fundamentals of hypnosis are as old as the human brain itself, and possibly much older. However, it wasn't until the 18th and 19th centuries that Western doctors started recognizing the power of hypnotic trance. At the time, it was used to "cure" a number of elements, and to sedate patients for surgery.

Since then, hypnotism has grown into a tool for therapy, pain relief, spiritual growth, and even entertainment. Psychological researchers continue to study the limits and effects of the hypnotic phenomenon today, using modern technology to detect brainwave functions and better understand what happens when humans go into a trance.

#2
Can Anyone be Hypnotized?

Generally speaking, yes. With very few exceptions, any person over the age of 10 or 12 can be brought into a hypnotic trance with their cooperation (remember, the hypnotist is working *with* a subject, not *on* them). While there are certain types of brain injuries and disabilities that make it nearly impossible to hypnotize a subject, these are exceedingly rare.

Putting those special cases aside, some people are more or less mentally flexible, making them better or worse candidates for hypnosis. However, with enough time and effort, any subject can benefit from going into a trance resource state. If you're reading this book, you can almost certainly use hypnosis to improve your life in any number of ways.

#3
How Long Does it Take to Fall Into a Hypnotic Trance?

There is no set answer this question because a great deal depends on the subject, situation, and context. Professional hypnotists often use rapid and even "instant" inductions designed to pull people into hypnotic trance for entertainment purposes. In those situations, someone may become hypnotized in a matter of seconds.

Hypnotherapists will typically spend longer with their subjects, pulling them into a deeper and more relaxed trance over the course of several minutes, or even longer if they need to try several different approaches. No matter how long the induction lasts, though, it is almost always the case that the subject will fall into hypnosis deeper and faster with each subsequent session. That is, the more times you are hypnotized, the greater the effects and benefits.

#4
What Does it Feel Like to be Hypnotized?

Different hypnotic subjects have unique experiences, but almost all report hypnosis being one of the most pleasant and relaxing experiences of their lives. Many report that they come back from a trance feeling as if they had just slept more peacefully than they have in years.

Aside from that, some hypnotic subjects will have a full memory of their session, while others remember little at all. In some cases, the hypnotist may use careful suggestions to ensure that the details remain completely clear. However, regardless of the circumstances, nearly everyone who is hypnotized finds it to be highly enjoyable and would be happy to participate again in the future.

#5
Are Hypnotized People Really Under Someone Else's Control?

In a stage hypnosis setting, it may appear as if the subjects are under the complete control of the hypnotist who is offering suggestions. However, this is largely an illusion. For one thing, each of the subjects has consented to be part of the show. And for another thing, their subconscious minds are still working to prevent them from coming to harm.

So, although the reactions you see may be entertaining and dramatized, hypnotic subjects generally won't do anything under a trance that they wouldn't do in everyday life. They certainly won't violate their own sense of safety or ethics, regardless of any suggestion they may receive. It may appear as if hypnotic subjects are under control, but they are really acting out images and impressions being formed by their own minds.

#6
Can a Person be Hypnotized Without Knowing it?

There are really two answers to this question. Generally, when someone asks this, what they really want to know is whether the hypnotist can draw another person into a trance without their knowledge or consent. I assure them that this is very unlikely to happen, since hypnotists work together with their participants to induce a specific mental state. It's a partnership, not a magic spell.

However, most humans drift in and out of a hypnotic state several times throughout the day. You can be "unintentionally hypnotized" watching TV, playing video games, driving to work, and so on. None of these represents a formal hypnotic trance, but they are very similar from a mental perspective. You've probably been hypnotized already several times today, but that's nothing to be afraid of.

#7
Why is Hypnosis so Good for Treating Addictions and Anxieties?

Given that there are so many different programs and medications out there to treat everyday problems, some people find it surprising that anyone would turn to hypnosis. However, not only is it faster, cheaper, and safer to break addictions and bad habits with the power of your mind, it can also be more effective.

To understand why, consider the mental reframing that occurs when someone uses hypnotherapy to give up smoking. In a very short period of time, they go from feeling like a smoker to a non-smoker. In other words, they don't go through the pain and withdrawal of quitting; they simply lose the urge to enjoy nicotine in the first place. If you can change the way you feel about something subconsciously, it can have very powerful and long-lasting results.

#8
What Else Can Hypnosis be Used For?

There aren't many limits on what you can improve in your life using self-hypnosis or hypnotherapy. In addition to addictions and anxieties, hypnosis can be used to treat weight loss, low self-esteem, bad eating habits, and insomnia. People have used hypnotism to ease physical pain, get past psychological or emotional trauma, and even cure certain types of sexual dysfunction.

Additionally, even though many people focus on the problems that can be solved with hypnosis, it's important not to overlook the positive things that can be achieved. Hypnotism can help with goal setting of any kind in your personal or professional life. You don't have to quit anything to make money, be a better salesperson, learn a new skill, or become more active. And yet, these can be among the best ways to redirect your subconscious mind.

#9
Can I Hypnotize Myself?

Absolutely. In fact, with time and practice, you may be your own best hypnotist. Not only is it inexpensive to work with yourself hypnotically, but it gives you the chance to write your own scripts and set your own agenda. It's also true that some individuals feel more comfortable experimenting with hypnosis on their own because they fear being under another person's guidance.

Although some people prefer to work with a professional hypnotherapist to break bad habits and move their lives forward, even a professional might advise follow-up work that's either self-guided or dependent on a recording. The bottom line is that if you have a few minutes, a quiet spot to sit, and a desire to reach your subconscious mind, you certainly can hypnotize yourself.

#10
How Can I Learn Hypnosis?

There are any number of places you can learn more about hypnosis. As with everything in life, however, what you get from the process will depend a great deal on the quality of the educational materials you have to work with. Although there are lots of online courses that promise to make you a "master hypnotist" within hours, it's good to learn from reputable sources with the right credentials.

This is particularly true if you plan to work with others on a therapeutic basis. Depending on where you live, you may need to show that you've passed an accredited course and earned a government license to practice hypnotherapy. And even if your local regulations aren't that stringent, it's never a bad idea to get a bit of expert instruction if you're committed to helping others lead happier, healthier lives.

HAPPINESS IS A CHOICE

THERE so many books written and produced every year that no single person could even read a small percentage of them. In fact, most of us can't make the time to read the things that are written about topics that particularly interest us, or are relevant to our jobs.

I mention this for a couple of reasons. The first is that if you've made it all the way to the end of this particular book, I want to both congratulate and thank you. I hope the information you've found within its pages will make a positive impact on your life. I've done what I could to keep the information brief and to-the-point. I know you don't have a lot of time, and even if you did there would be a lot more to read.

The other reason I bring this up is that, despite all the knowledge that's being shared online and off, it seems that many of us find the all-important topic of happiness more elusive than ever. We have many sources of information, but struggle to find answers.

While nothing I've given you in the preceding chapters is *complicated*, it's all *effective*. Your subconscious really does play a major role in setting your moods, attitude, and perspective. If you can point this part of your mind in the right direction, it can guide you towards the kind of success that doesn't just show up on a business card or bank statement. Train yourself to get what you really want and need, and you can actually be happier.

Shouldn't that be the goal of every book? What is achievement without a sense of peace and fulfillment? These are questions I ask myself when I sit down to write, and I hope you'll feel like I've given you satisfactory answers along the way. We all feel better when we're happier and being driven to fulfill an important purpose or achieve something we've been dreaming about for a long time. Conversely, we are less happy when we feel like we're floundering and out of control in our own lives.

Now you know what it takes to choose a target that's meaningful to you, and then to hypnotize yourself until your subconscious mind brings you the result you've been looking for. That's bound to make you happier, and even if it doesn't, you can start the process all over again for a *different* goal until you are.

The human mind is an amazing thing, and most people don't put it to its best uses. My hope is that you'll take the advice I've humbly offered you in this book and put it to work right away. Once you do, I hope you'll contact me and let me know what kind of positive difference it has made. I can't wait to hear about your success!

ABOUT THE AUTHOR

JASON Christopher is a hypnotist, magician, and motivational speaker. For more than two decades, he's been putting together keynotes and workshops that are as engaging and thought-provoking as they are hilarious.

All of Jason's speeches and learning materials focus on the art of personal self-improvement. Using hypnosis, sleight-of-hand, and a heavy dose of humor, he guides readers and listeners through the process change that can result in losing weight, controlling pain, cutting back on stress, or improving memory and concentration. As a result, he has become a favorite presenter for corporations, universities, and civic groups throughout North America.

A graduate of Robert Morris College, Jason currently lives in Pittsburgh, PA. When he is not speaking and performing, enjoy spending time with his family and playing tennis as well as making (and drinking) wine.